李
太
白
集

Selected

Poems

of

Li Po

First Warbler Classics Edition 2025

English translations, introduction, and afterword first appeared in *The Jade Mountain*
published by Alfred A. Knopf, New York, in 1929.

Biographical Note by Bob Holman & Margery Snyder first published by
ThoughtCo. in 2019. Printed with permission.

warblerpress.com

ISBN 978-1-965684-45-0 (paperback)
ISBN 978-1-965684-46-7 (ebook)

李太白集

Selected
Poems
of
Li Po

warbler classics

"Literature endures like the universal spirit,
And its breath becomes a part of the vitals of all men."

LI SHANG-YIN

CONTENTS

POETRY AND CULTURE
by Witter Bynner

L IKE MOST OF us who have been schooled in this western
world, I was afforded in my youth a study of culture flowing
mainly from two sources, the Greek and the Hebrew. I had come
to feel that poetic literature must contain streams from one or
the other of these two sources: on the one hand the clean, objec-
tive, symmetrical, athletic beauty of the Greek; on the other
hand the turgid, subjective, distorted, elaborated beauty of the
Hebrew. Like my fellow students, I had been offered nothing of
the literatures of the Far East. I am still doubtful that I could
ever feel any real adherence to the ornate and entranced liter-
ature of India; but I have come by accident into as close touch
with Chinese poetry as a westerner is able to come without a
knowledge of the Chinese tongue. And I feel with conviction
that in the matter of poetry I have begun to receive a new, finer,
and deeper education than ever came to me from the Hebrew
or the Greek.

Centuries ago cultivated Chinese had reached the intellectual
saturation which has tired the mind of the modern European.
The Chinese gentleman knew the ancient folk-songs, compiled
by Confucius. He knew also, all around him, a profoundly rich
civilization, a more poised and particularized sophistication

than we westerners have yet attained. Through the Asian centuries everyone has written verse. In fact, from early imperial days down to these even worse disordered days of the Republic, the sense of poetry as a natural and solacing part of life has lasted among the Chinese people. Whether or not the individual may form or enjoy his poetry in metrical shape, he is constantly aware of the kinship between the beauty of the world and the beauty of imaginative phrase. On any Chinese mountain-climb toward a temple, rock after rock with its terse and suggestive inscription will bear witness to this temper. So will the street cries of the peddlers, or the names of the tea-houses, and on many hill-tops and lake-sides the casual but reverent jottings of this or that anonymous appreciator of natural beauty. When Whitman said: "To have great poets there must be great audiences too," he must have had in the back of his mind enriched generations like the Elizabethan in England or like almost any generation in China. In those great audiences each man, to the limit of his capacity and with natural ease, was a poet.

There is a simple secret in these generations. It is told in a pamphlet by a venerable Chinese scholar who, until his death two years ago, was still with infinite passion adhering to the precepts of his ancestors, and with infinite patience, acceptably expressed by the way among foreigners, adhering to his conviction that foreigners impair the health of China. His name is Ku Hungming. His pamphlet, written in English, one of the five languages which he could use, is called *The Spirit of the Chinese People*. In it he advances, as reason for the eternal youth of the Chinese people, the fact that the average Chinese has managed to maintain within himself the head of a man and the heart of a child. On this brief he is absorbingly interesting, explaining the continuance of Chinese culture, the only ancient culture still racially existent. My immediate concern with his brief is more special. I detect in it something that he does not specify: a reason for the continuance of poetry as a live factor among his people and, more than that, the best reason I know of for the persistence of poetry anywhere among cultured races.

Music may be the most intimate of the arts, I am not sure. Except for simple melodies, music is beyond the reach of any individual who is not a technician. Painting and sculpture are obviously arts expressing themselves in single given objects, which, although they may be copied and so circulated, are for the most part accessible only to the privileged or to those who make pilgrimages. Poetry more than any other of the arts may be carried about by a man either in his own remembering heart or else in compact and easily available printed form. It belongs to anyone. It is of all the arts the closest to a man; and it will so continue to be, in spite of the apparent shocks given it by the noises of modern commerce and science and jazz.

It has been a common occurrence in China that poets, even the best of them, devote their earlier years to some form of public service. Century after century, Chinese poems reflect this deep devotion of their authors to the good of the State—their unwavering allegiance to righteousness, even when it meant demotion or exile or death. In modern western times there have been periods when poetry has seemed to be a candle-lit and thin-blooded occupation. I venture to surmise that poetry written in that sort of atmosphere grows with time less and less valid, less and less noticed. As a matter of fact, the outstanding English poets have been acutely concerned with the happiness of their fellow men and have given themselves warmly to public causes in which they believed. Similarly, present-day poets in America, with amazingly few exceptions, have clustered to the defence of noble souls at bay like Eugene Debs, or have been quick to protest against doubtful justice, as in the case of Sacco and Vanzetti. This sort of zeal may not result in poetry of a high order immediately connected with the specific cause; but there is no question that but for this bravery, this heat on behalf of man's better nature, there would not be in the hearts of the poets so fine a crucible for their more personal alchemies.

Let me say a more general word than Dr. Kiang's as to the characteristic method of the best Chinese poetry. I am not referring to the technical means by which a Chinese poet makes his words balanced and melodious. The discovery which has largely undone my previous convictions as to the way of writing poetry has rather to do with use of substance than with turns of expression. Mencius said long ago, in reference to the Odes collected by Confucius: "Those who explain the Odes must not insist on one term so as to do violence to a sentence, nor on a sentence so as to do violence to the general scope. They must try with their thoughts to meet that scope, and then they will apprehend it." In the poetry of the west we are accustomed to let our appreciative minds accept with joy this or that passage in a poem—to prefer the occasional glitter of a jewel to the straight light of the sun. The Chinese poet seldom lets any portion of what he is saying unbalance the entirety. Moreover, with the exception of a particular class of writing—adulatory verse written for the court—Chinese poetry rarely trespasses beyond the bounds of actuality. Whereas western poets will take actualities as points of departure for exaggeration or fantasy, or else as shadows of contrast against dreams of unreality, the great Chinese poets accept the world exactly as they find it in all its terms, and with profound simplicity find therein sufficient solace. Even in phraseology they seldom talk about one thing in terms of another, but are able enough and sure enough as artists to make the ultimately exact terms become the beautiful terms. If a metaphor is used, it is a metaphor directly relating to the theme, not something borrowed from the ends of the earth. The metaphor must be concurrent with the action or flow of the poem; not merely superinduced, but an integral part of both the scene and the emotion.

Wordsworth, of our poets, comes closest to the Chinese; but their poetry cleaves even nearer to nature than his. They perform the miracle of identifying the wonder of beauty with common sense. Rather, they prove that the simplest common sense, the most salutary, and the most nearly universal, is the sense of the beauty of nature, quickened and yet sobered by the wistful warmth of human friendship.

For our taste, used as we are to the operatic in poetry, the substance of Chinese poems seems often mild or even trivial; but if we will be honest with ourselves and with our appreciation of what is lastingly important, we shall find these very same poems to be momentous details in the immense patience of beauty. They are the heart of an intimate letter. They bring the true, the beautiful, the everlasting, into simple, easy touch with the human, the homely, and the immediate. And I predict that future western poets will go to school with the masters of the T'ang Dynasty, as well as with the masters of the golden age of Greece, or with the Hebrew prophets, or with the English dramatists or romanticists—to learn how best may be expressed, for themselves and others, that passionate patience which is the core of life.

It is not necessary that culture bring about the death of poetry, as it did in the Rome of Virgil. The cynics are wrong who see in our future no place for an art which belongs, they say, to the childhood of the race. The head of a man and the heart of a child working together as in the Chinese have made possible with one race and may make possible with any race, even in the thick of the most intricate culture, the continuance of the purest poetry.

Because of the absence of tenses, of personal pronouns and of connectives generally, the translator of Chinese poetry, like the Chinese reader himself, has considerable leeway as to interpretation. If even in English, so much more definite a language, there may be varying interpretations of a given poem, it is no wonder that critics and annotators have differed as to the meaning of poems in Chinese. There have been frequent instances in this volume where Dr. Kiang and I have discussed several possible meanings of a poem and have chosen for translation into the more definite language the meaning we preferred.

With his sanction I have decided that for readers in English it is better to eliminate or use only seldom the names of places and persons not highly important to the sense of a poem: to use "southern" or "eastern," for instance, instead of regional names unfamiliar in the Occident; to indicate the person meant when the poem, according to Chinese custom, employs the name and attributes of some other similar well-known person, and to embody in the English text something of the significance which would be conveyed to any Chinese reader, but not to western readers, by historical or literary allusions.

At the risk of criticism, I have made certain reasonable

compromises. I have used the sometimes inaccurate term "Tartar" instead of "Hun" or "barbarian," the term "China" instead of "Han," the term "Turkestan" when it roughly corresponded to the ancient term. There are many other approximations which have seemed advisable. Once in a while, for good reason, I have changed a title. And there are occasional unimportant omissions. I have omitted, for instance, the "ninth-born" or "eleventhborn," frequently added in the original to names of persons, and meaning the ninth or eleventh child in a family. Whenever possible, I have avoided phraseology which, natural and familiar in Chinese, would be exotic or quaint in English; I have hoped rather to accent in these T'ang masterpieces the human and universal qualities by which they have endured.

WITTER BYNNER
Santa Fe, New Mexico, 1929

李
太
白
集

Selected
Poems
of
Li Po

静夜思

床前明月光,
疑是地上霜。
舉頭望明月,
低頭思故鄉。

In the Quiet Night

So bright a gleam on the foot of my bed—
Could there have been a frost already?
Lifting myself to look, I found that it was moonlight.
Sinking back again, I thought suddenly of home.

怨情

美人捲珠簾，
深坐顰蛾眉。
但見淚痕濕，
不知心恨誰。

A Bitter Love

How beautiful she looks, opening the pearly casement,
And how quiet she leans, and how troubled her brow is!
You may see the tears now, bright on her cheek,
But not the man she so bitterly loves.

玉階怨

玉階生白露，
夜久侵羅襪。
卻下水晶簾，
玲瓏望秋月。

A Sigh from a Staircase of Jade
(Written to Music)

Her jade-white staircase is cold with dew;
Her silk soles are wet, she lingered there so long...
Behind her closed casement, why is she still waiting,
Watching through its crystal pane the glow of the autumn moon?

送孟浩然之廣陵

故人西辭黃鶴樓，
煙花三月下揚州。
孤帆遠影碧空盡，
惟見長江天際流。

A Farewell to Mêng Hao-Jan on His Way to Yang-Chou

You have left me behind, old friend, at the Yellow Crane Terrace,
On your way to visit Yang-chou in the misty month of flowers;
Your sail, a single shadow, becomes one with the blue sky,
Till now I see only the river, on its way to heaven.

早發白帝城

朝辭白帝彩雲間，
千里江陵一日還。
兩岸猿聲啼不住，
輕舟已過萬重山。

Through the Yang-tze Gorges

From the walls of Po-ti high in the coloured dawn
To Kiang-ling by night-fall is three hundred miles,
Yet monkeys are still calling on both banks behind me
To my boat these ten thousand mountains away.

清平調詞三首

其一
雲想衣裳花想容，
春風拂檻露華濃。
若非羣玉山頭見，
會向瑤臺月下逢。

其二
一枝紅艷露凝香，
雲雨巫山枉斷腸。
借問漢宮誰得似，
可憐飛燕倚新妝

其三
名花傾國兩相歡，
長得君王帶笑看。
解釋春風無限恨，
沉香亭北倚闌干。

A Song of Pure Happiness
(Written to Music for Lady Yang)

I

Her robe is a cloud, her face a flower;
Her balcony, glimmering with the bright spring dew,
Is either the tip of earth's Jade Mountain
Or a moon-edged roof of paradise.

II

There's a perfume stealing moist from a shaft of red blossom,
And a mist, through the heart, from the magical Hill of Wu—
The palaces of China have never known such beauty—
Not even Flying Swallow with all her glittering garments.

III

Lovely now together, his lady and his flowers
Lighten for ever the Emperor's eye,
As he listens to the sighing of the far spring wind
Where she leans on a railing in the Aloe Pavilion.

贈孟浩然

吾愛孟夫子，風流天下聞。
紅顏棄軒冕，白首臥松雲。
醉月頻中聖，迷花不事君。
高山安可仰，徒此揖清芬。

A Message to Mêng Hao-Jan

Master, I hail you from my heart,
And your fame arisen to the skies....
Renouncing in ruddy youth the importance of hat and chariot,
You chose pine-trees and clouds; and now, white-haired,
Drunk with the moon, a sage of dreams,
Flower-bewitched, you are deaf to the Emperor...
High mountain, how I long to reach you,
Breathing your sweetness even here!

渡荊門送別

渡遠荊門外，來從楚國遊。
山隨平野盡，江入大荒流。
月下飛天鏡，雲生結海樓。
仍憐故鄉水，萬里送行舟。

Bidding a Friend Farewell at Ching-Men Ferry

Sailing far off from Ching-men Ferry,
Soon you will be with people in the south,
Where the mountains end and the plains begin
And the river winds through wilderness....
The moon is lifted like a mirror,
Sea-clouds gleam like palaces,
And the water has brought you a touch of home
To draw your boat three hundred miles.

送友人

青山橫北郭，白水繞東城。
此地一為別，孤蓬萬里征。
浮雲遊子意，落日故人情。
揮手自茲去，蕭蕭班馬鳴。

A Farewell to a Friend

With a blue line of mountains north of the wall,
And east of the city a white curve of water,
Here you must leave me and drift away
Like a loosened water-plant hundreds of miles....
I shall think of you in a floating cloud;
So in the sunset think of me.
...We wave our hands to say good-bye,
And my horse is neighing again and again.

聽蜀僧濬彈琴

蜀僧抱綠綺，西下峨眉峰。
為我一揮手，如聽萬壑松。
客心洗流水，餘響入霜鍾。
不覺碧山暮，秋雲暗幾重。

On Hearing Chün the Buddhist Monk from Shu Play His Lute

The monk from Shu with his green silk lute-case,
Walking west down O-mêi Mountain,
Has brought me by one touch of the strings
The breath of pines in a thousand valleys.
I hear him in the cleansing brook,
I hear him in the icy bells;
And I feel no change though the mountain darkens
And cloudy autumn heaps the sky.

夜泊牛渚懷古

牛渚西江夜，青天無片雲。
登舟望秋月，空憶謝將軍。
余亦能高詠，斯人不可聞。
明朝掛帆席，楓葉落紛紛。

Thought of Old Time from a Night-Mooring Under Mount Niu-Chu

This night to the west of the river-brim
There is not one cloud in the whole blue sky,
As I watch from my deck the autumn moon,
Vainly remembering old General Hsieh....
I have poems; I can read;
He heard others, but not mine.
...Tomorrow I shall hoist my sail.
With fallen maple-leaves behind me.

登金陵鳳凰臺

鳳凰臺上鳳凰遊，鳳去臺空江自流。
吳宮花草埋幽徑，晉代衣冠成古丘。
三山半落青天外，二水中分白鷺洲。
總為浮雲能蔽日，長安不見使人愁。

On Climbing in Nan-King to the Terrace of Phoenixes

Phoenixes that played here once, so that the place was named
    for them,
Have abandoned it now to this desolate river;
The paths of Wu Palace are crooked with weeds;
The garments of Chin are ancient dust.
...Like this green horizon halving the Three Peaks,
Like this Island of White Egrets dividing the river,
A cloud has arisen between the Light of Heaven and me,
To hide his city from my melancholy heart.

下終南山過斛斯山人宿置酒

暮從碧山下，山月隨人歸。
卻顧所來徑，蒼蒼橫翠微。
相攜及田家，童稚開荊扉。
綠竹入幽徑，青蘿拂行衣。
歡言得所憩，美酒聊共揮。
長歌吟松風，曲盡河星稀。
我醉君復樂，陶然共忘機。

44

Down Chung-Nan Mountain to the Kind Pillow and Bowl of
Hu Ssü

Down the blue mountain in the evening,
Moonlight was my homeward escort.
Looking back, I saw my path
Lie in levels of deep shadow. . .
I was passing the farm-house of a friend,
When his children called from a gate of thorn
And led me twining through jade bamboos
Where green vines caught and held my clothes.
And I was glad of a chance to rest
And glad of a chance to drink with my friend....
We sang to the tune of the wind in the pines;
And we finished our songs as the stars went down,
When, I being drunk and my friend more than happy.
Between us we forgot the world.

月下獨酌

花間一壺酒，獨酌無相親。
舉杯邀明月，對影成三人。
月既不解飲，影徒隨我身。
暫伴月將影，行樂須及春。
我歌月徘徊，我舞影零亂。
醒時同交歡，醉後各分散。
永結無情遊，相期邈雲漢。

Drinking Alone with the Moon

From a pot of wine among the flowers I drank alone.
There was no one with me—
Till, raising my cup, I asked the bright moon
To bring me my shadow and make us three.
Alas, the moon was unable to drink
And my shadow tagged me vacantly;
But still for a while I had these friends
To cheer me through the end of spring....
I sang. The moon encouraged me.
I danced. My shadow tumbled after.
As long as I knew, we were boon companions.
And then I was drunk, and we lost one another.
....Shall goodwill ever be secure?
I watch the long road of the River of Stars.

春思

燕草如碧絲，秦桑低綠枝。
當君懷歸日，是妾斷腸時。
春風不相識，何事入羅幃。

In Spring

Your grasses up north are as blue as jade,
Our mulberries here curve green-threaded branches;
And at last you think of returning home,
Now when my heart is almost broken....
O breeze of the spring, since I dare not know you,
Why part the silk curtains by my bed?

關山月

明月出天山，蒼茫雲海間。
長風幾萬里，吹度玉門關。
漢下白登道，胡窺青海灣。
由來征戰地，不見有人還。
戍客望邊邑，思歸多苦顏。
高樓當此夜，歎息未應閑。

The Moon at the Fortified Pass
(Written to Music)

The bright moon lifts from the Mountain of Heaven
In an infinite haze of cloud and sea.
And the wind, that has come a thousand miles,
Beats at the Jade Pass battlements....
China marches its men down Po-têng Road
While Tartar troops peer across blue waters of the bay
And since not one battle famous in history
Sent all its fighters back again,
The soldiers turn round, looking toward the border,
And think of home, with wistful eyes,
And of those tonight in the upper chambers
Who toss and sigh and cannot rest.

子夜吳歌　秋歌

長安一片月，萬戶擣衣聲。
秋風吹不盡，總是玉關情。
何日平胡虜，良人罷遠征。

A Song of an Autumn Midnight
(Written to a Su-chou Melody)

A slip of the moon hangs over the capital;
Ten thousand washing-mallets are pounding;
And the autumn wind is blowing my heart
For ever and ever toward the Jade Pass....
Oh, when will the Tartar troops be conquered,
And my husband come back from the long campaign!

長幹行

妾髮初覆額，折花門前劇。
郎騎竹馬來，遶牀弄青梅。
同居長干里，兩小無嫌猜。
十四為君婦，羞顏未嘗開。
低頭向暗壁，千喚不一迴。
十五始展眉，願同塵與灰。
常存抱柱信，豈上望夫臺。
十六君遠行，瞿塘灩澦堆。
五月不可觸，猿聲天上哀。
門前遲行跡，一一生綠苔。
苔深不能掃，落葉秋風早。
八月胡蝶來，雙飛西園草。
感此傷妾心，坐愁紅顏老。
早晚下三巴，預將書報家。
相迎不道遠，直至長風沙。

Song of Ch'ang-Kan
(Written to Music)

My hair had hardly covered my forehead.
I was picking flowers, playing by my door,
When you, my lover, on a bamboo horse,
Came trotting in circles and throwing green plums.
We lived near together on a lane in Ch'ang-kan,
Both of us young and happy-hearted.
...At fourteen I became your wife,
So bashful that I dared not smile,
And I lowered my head toward a dark corner
And would not turn to your thousand calls;
But at fifteen I straightened my brows and laughed,
Learning that no dust could ever seal our love.
That even unto death I would await you by my post
And would never lose heart in the tower of silent watching.
...Then when I was sixteen, you left on a long journey
Through the Gorges of Ch'ü-t'ang, of rock and whirling water.
And then came the Fifth-month, more than I could bear.
And I tried to hear the monkeys in your lofty far-off sky.
Your footprints by our door, where I had watched you go,
Were hidden, every one of them, under green moss.
Hidden under moss too deep to sweep away.

And the first autumn wind added fallen leaves.
And now, in the Eighth-month, yellowing butterflies
Hover, two by two, in our west-garden grasses....
And, because of all this, my heart is breaking
And I fear for my bright cheeks, lest they fade.
...Oh, at last, when you return through the three Pa districts,
Send me a message home ahead!
And I will come and meet you and will never mind the distance,
All the way to Chang-fêng Sha.

廬山謠寄盧侍御虛舟

我本楚狂人，鳳歌笑孔丘。
手持綠玉杖，朝別黃鶴樓。
五嶽尋仙不辭遠，一生好入名山遊。
廬山秀出南斗傍，屏風九疊雲錦張，
影落明湖青黛光。
金闕前開二峰長，銀河倒掛三石梁，
香爐瀑布遙相望，迴崖沓嶂凌蒼蒼。
翠影紅霞映朝日，鳥飛不到吳天長。
登高壯觀天地間，大江茫茫去不還。
黃雲萬里動風色，白波九道流雪山。
好爲廬山謠，興因廬山發。
閑窺石鏡清我心，謝公行處蒼苔沒。
早服還丹無世情，琴心三疊道初成。
遙見仙人綵雲裏，手把芙蓉朝玉京。
先期汗漫九垓上，願接盧敖遊太清。

A Song of Lu Mountain

To Censor Lu Hsü-chou I am the madman of the Ch'u country
Who sang a mad song disputing Confucius.
...Holding in my hand a staff of green jade,
I have crossed, since morning at the Yellow Crane Terrace,
All five Holy Mountains, without a thought of distance,
According to the one constant habit of my life.
...Lu Mountain stands beside the Southern Dipper
In clouds reaching silken like a nine-panelled screen,
With its shadows in a crystal lake deepening the green water.
The Golden Gate opens into two mountain-ranges.
A silver stream is hanging down to three stone bridges
Within sight of the mighty Tripod Falls.
Ledges of cliff and winding trails lead to blue sky
And a flush of cloud in the morning sun,
Whence no flight of birds could be blown into Wu.
...I climb to the top. I survey the whole world.
I see the long river that runs beyond return,
Yellow clouds that winds have driven hundreds of miles
And a snow-peak whitely circled by the swirl of a ninefold
    stream.
And so I am singing a song of Lu Mountain,
A song that is born of the breath of Lu Mountain.

…Where the Stone Mirror makes the heart's purity purer
And green moss has buried the footsteps of Hsieh,
I have eaten the immortal pellet and, rid of the world's troubles,
Before the lute's third playing have achieved my element.
Far away I watch the angels riding coloured clouds
Toward heaven's Jade City, with hibiscus in their hands.
And so, when I have traversed the nine sections of the world,
I will follow Saint Lu-ao up the Great Purity.

夢遊天姥吟留別

海客談瀛洲，煙濤微茫信難求。
越人語天姥，雲霞明滅或可覩。
天姥連天向天橫，勢拔五嶽掩赤城。
天台四萬八千丈，對此欲倒東南傾。
我欲因之夢吳越，一夜飛度鏡湖月。
湖月照我影，送我至剡溪。
謝公宿處今尚在，淥水蕩漾清猨啼。
腳著謝公屐，身登青雲梯。
半壁見海日，空中聞天雞。
千巖萬轉路不定，迷花倚石忽已暝。
熊咆龍吟殷巖泉，慄深林兮驚層巔。
雲青青兮欲雨，水澹澹兮生煙。
列缺霹靂，丘巒崩摧。
洞天石扉，訇然中開。
青冥浩蕩不見底，日月照耀金銀臺。
霓為衣兮風為馬，雲之君兮紛紛而來下。
虎鼓瑟兮鸞迴車，仙之人兮列如麻。
忽魂悸以魄動，怳驚起而長嗟。
惟覺時之枕席，失向來之煙霞。
世間行樂亦如此，古來萬事東流水。
別君去兮何時還？且放白鹿青崖間，須行即騎訪
　　名山。
安能摧眉折腰事權貴，使我不得開心顏。

T'ien-Mu Mountain Ascended in a Dream

A seafaring visitor will talk about Japan,
Which waters and mists conceal beyond approach;
But Yüeh people talk about Heavenly Mother Mountain,
Still seen through its varying deepnesses of cloud.
In a straight line to heaven, its summit enters heaven,
Tops the five Holy Peaks, and casts a shadow through China.
With the hundred-mile length of the Heavenly Terrace Range,
Which, just at this point, begins turning southeast.
…My heart and my dreams are in Wu and Yüeh
And they cross Mirror Lake all night in the moon.
And the moon lights my shadow
And me to Shan River—
With the hermitage of Hsieh still there
And the monkeys calling clearly over ripples of green water.
I wear his pegged boots
Up a ladder of blue cloud.
Sunny ocean half-way.
Holy cock-crow in space,
Myriad peaks and more valleys and nowhere a road.
Flowers lure me, rocks ease me. Day suddenly ends.
Bears, dragons, tempestuous on mountain and river,
Startle the forest and make the heights tremble.

Clouds darken with darkness of rain,
Streams pale with pallor of mist.
The Gods of Thunder and Lightning
Shatter the whole range.
The stone gate breaks asunder
Venting in the pit of heaven,
An impenetrable shadow.
...But now the sun and moon illumine a gold and silver terrace,
And, clad in rainbow garments, riding on the wind,
Come the queens of all the clouds, descending one by one.
With tigers for their lute-players and phoenixes for dancers.
Row upon row, like fields of hemp, range the fairy figures....
I move, my soul goes flying,
I wake with a long sigh,
My pillow and my matting
Are the lost clouds I was in.
...And this is the way it always is with human joy:
Ten thousand things run for ever like water toward the east.
And so I take my leave of you, not knowing for how long.
...But let me, on my green slope, raise a white deer
And ride to you, great mountain, when I have need of you.
Oh, how can I gravely bow and scrape to men of high rank and
     men of high office
Who never will suffer being shown an honest-hearted face!

金陵酒肆留別

風吹柳花滿店香，吳姬壓酒勸客嘗；
金陵子弟來相送，欲行不行各盡觴。
請君試問東流水，別意與之誰短長？

Parting at a Wine-Shop in Nan-King

A wind, bringing willow-cotton, sweetens the shop,
And a girl from Wu, pouring wine, urges me to share it
With my comrades of the city who are here to see me off;
And as each of them drains his cup, I say to him in parting.
Oh, go and ask this river running to the east
If it can travel farther than a friend's love!

宣州謝朓樓餞別校書叔雲

棄我去者，昨日之日不可留。
亂我心者，今日之日多煩憂。
長風萬里送秋雁，對此可以酣高樓。
蓬萊文章建安骨，中間小謝又清發。
俱懷逸興壯思飛，欲上青天覽明月。
抽刀斷水水更流，舉杯銷愁愁更愁。
人生在世不稱意，明朝散髮弄扁舟。

A Farewell to Secretary Shu-Yün at the Hsieh T'iao Villa in
Hsüan-Chou

Since yesterday had to throw me and bolt,
Today has hurt my heart even more.
The autumn wildgeese have a long wind for escort
As I face them from this villa, drinking my wine.
The bones of great writers are your brushes, in the School of
    Heaven,
And I am a Lesser Hsieh growing up by your side.
We both are exalted to distant thought,
Aspiring to the sky and the bright moon.
But since water still flows, though we cut it with our swords.
And sorrows return, though we drown them with wine,
Since the world can in no way answer our craving,
I will loosen my hair tomorrow and take to a fishing-boat.

蜀道難

噫，吁嚱，危乎高哉！
蜀道之難，難於上青天！
蠶叢及魚鳧，開國何茫然！
爾來四萬八千歲，不與秦塞通人煙。
西當太白有鳥道，可以橫絕峨眉巔。
地崩山摧壯士死，然後天梯石棧相鉤連。
上有六龍回日之高標，下有衝波逆折之回川，
黃鶴之飛尚不得過，猿猱欲度愁攀緣。
青泥何盤盤，百步九折縈巖巒。
捫參歷井仰脅息，以手撫膺坐長歎！
問君西遊何時還？畏途巉巖不可攀。
但見悲鳥號古木，雄飛雌從繞林間；
又聞子規啼夜月，愁空山。
蜀道之難，難於上青天，使人聽此凋朱顏！
連峰去天不盈尺，枯松倒掛倚絕壁，
飛湍瀑流爭喧豗，砯崖轉石萬壑雷。
其險也如此，嗟爾遠道之人胡為乎來哉！
劍閣崢嶸而崔嵬，一夫當關，萬夫莫開。
所守或匪親，化為狼與豺，
朝避猛虎，夕避長蛇，磨牙吮血，殺人如麻。
錦城雖云樂，不如早還家。
蜀道之難，難於上青天！側身西望長咨嗟。

Hard Roads in Shu
(Written to Music)

Oh, but it is high and very dangerous!
Such travelling is harder than scaling the blue sky.
…Until two rulers of this region
Pushed their way through in the misty ages,
Forty-eight thousand years had passed
With nobody arriving across the Ch'in border.
And the Great White Mountain, westward, still has only a bird's
    path
Up to the summit of O-mêi Peak—
Which was broken once by an earthquake and there were brave
    men lost,
Just finishing the stone rungs of their ladder toward heaven.
…High, as on a tall flag, six dragons drive the sun,
While the river, far below, lashes its twisted course.
Such height would be hard going for even a yellow crane,
So pity the poor monkeys who have only paws to use.
The Mountain of Green Clay is formed of many circles—
Each hundred steps, we have to turn nine turns among its
    mounds.
Panting, we brush Orion and pass the Well Star,
Then, holding our chests with our hands and sinking to the
    ground with a groan,

We wonder if this westward trail will never have an end.
The formidable path ahead grows darker, darker still,
With nothing heard but the call of birds hemmed in by the
  ancient forest,
Male birds smoothly wheeling, following the females;
And there come to us the melancholy voices of the cuckoos
Out on the empty mountain, under the lonely moon...
Such travelling is harder than scaling the blue sky.
Even to hear of it turns the cheek pale.
With the highest crag barely a foot below heaven.
Dry pines hang, head down, from the face of the cliffs,
And a thousand plunging cataracts outroar one another
And send through ten thousand valleys a thunder of spinning
  stones.
With all this danger upon danger,
Why do people come here who live at a safe distance?
...Though Dagger-Tower Pass be firm and grim,
 And while one man guards it
Ten thousand cannot force it,
What if he be not loyal,
But a wolf toward his fellows?
...There are ravenous tigers to fear in the day
And venomous reptiles in the night
With their teeth and their fangs ready
To cut people down like hemp.
...Though the City of Silk be delectable, I would rather turn
  home quickly.
Such travelling is harder than scaling the blue sky...
But I still face westward with a dreary moan.

長相思

其一
長相思，在長安，
絡緯秋啼金井闌，微霜淒淒簟色寒。
孤燈不明思欲絕，卷帷望月空長歎，美人如花隔
　　雲端。
上有青冥之長天，下有淥水之波瀾。
天長路遠魂飛苦，夢魂不到關山難。
長相思，摧心肝。

其二
日色欲盡花含煙，月明如素愁不眠。
趙瑟初停鳳凰柱，蜀琴欲奏鴛鴦弦。
此曲有意無人傳，願隨春風寄燕然，憶君迢迢隔
　　青天。
昔日橫波目，今成流淚泉。
不信妾腸斷，歸來看取明鏡前。

Endless Yearning
(Written to Music)

I

"I am endlessly yearning
To be in Ch'ang-an.
...Insects hum of autumn by the gold brim of the well;
A thin frost glistens like little mirrors on my cold mat;
The high lantern flickers; and deeper grows my longing.
I lift the shade and, with many a sigh, gaze upon the moon,
Single as a flower, centred from the clouds.
Above, I see the blueness and deepness of sky.
Below, I see the greenness and the restlessness of water...
Heaven is high, earth wide; bitter between them flies my sorrow.
Can I dream through the gateway, over the mountain?
Endless longing
Breaks my heart."

II

"The sun has set, and a mist is in the flowers;
And the moon grows very white and people sad and sleepless.
A Chao harp has just been laid mute on its phoenix-holder.
And a Shu lute begins to sound its mandarin-duck strings...

Since nobody can bear to you the burden of my song,
Would that it might follow the spring wind to Yen-jan Mountain.
I think of you far away, beyond the blue sky,
And my eyes that once were sparkling
Are now a well of tears.
…Oh, if ever you should doubt this aching of my heart,
Here in my bright mirror come back and look at me! "

行路難

金樽清酒斗十千，玉盤珍羞直萬錢。
停杯投箸不能食，拔劍四顧心茫然。
欲渡黃河冰塞川，將登太行雪滿山。
閑來垂釣碧溪上，忽復乘舟夢日邊。
行路難！行路難！多歧路，今安在？
長風破浪會有時，直掛雲帆濟滄海。

The Hard Road
(Written to Music)

Pure wine costs, for the golden cup, ten thousand coppers a
    flagon,
And a jade plate of dainty food calls for a million coins.
I fling aside my food-sticks and cup, I cannot eat nor drink…
I pull out my dagger, I peer four ways in vain.
I would cross the Yellow River, but ice chokes the ferry;
I would climb the T'ai-hang Mountains, but the sky is blind with
    snow…
I would sit and poise a fishing-pole, lazy by a brook—
But I suddenly dream of riding a boat, sailing for the sun…
Journeying is hard.
Journeying is hard.
There are many turnings—Which am I to follow?…
I will mount a long wind some day and break the heavy waves
And set my cloudy sail straight and bridge the deep, deep sea.

將進酒

君不見黃河之水天上來，奔流到海不復回。
君不見高堂明鏡悲白髮，朝如青絲暮成雪。
人生得意須盡歡，莫使金樽空對月。
天生我材必有用，千金散盡還復來。
烹羊宰牛且為樂，會須一飲三百杯。
岑夫子，丹丘生，將進酒，君莫停。
與君歌一曲，請君為我傾耳聽。
鐘鼓饌玉不足貴，但願長醉不用醒。
古來聖賢皆寂寞，惟有飲者留其名。
陳王昔時宴平樂，斗酒十千恣歡謔。
主人何為言少錢，徑須沽取對君酌。
五花馬、千金裘，呼兒將出換美酒，與爾同銷萬
　古愁。

Bringing in the Wine
(Written to Music)

See how the Yellow River's waters move out of heaven.
Entering the ocean, never to return.
See how lovely locks in bright mirrors in high chambers,
Though silken-black at morning, have changed by night to snow.
...Oh, let a man of spirit venture where he pleases
And never tip his golden cup empty toward the moon!
Since heaven gave the talent, let it be employed!
Spin a thousand pieces of silver, all of them come back!
Cook a sheep, kill a cow, whet the appetite.
And make me, of three hundred bowls, one long drink!
...To the old master, Ts'ên,
And the young scholar, Tan-ch'iu,
Bring in the wine!
Let your cups never rest!
Let me sing you a song!
Let your ears attend!
What are bell and drum, rare dishes and treasure?
Let me be forever drunk and never come to reason!
Sober men of olden days and sages are forgotten,
And only the great drinkers are famous for all time.
...Prince Ch'ên paid at a banquet in the Palace of Perfection

Ten thousand coins for a cask of wine, with many a laugh and
   quip.
Why say, my host, that your money is gone?
Go and buy wine and we'll drink it together!
My flower-dappled horse,
My furs worth a thousand,
Hand them to the boy to exchange for good wine,
And we'll drown away the woes of ten thousand generations!

CHINESE POETRY
by Kiang Kang-hu

POEMS OF THE EARLY PERIOD

CHINESE POETRY BEGAN with our written history about 5500 years ago. The oldest poems now extant were written by the Emperor Yao (2357 B.C.); and one of them was adopted as the Chinese national song in the beginning of the Republic, because Yao was in reality a life president of the most ancient republic in the world, and this poem expresses the republican spirit. Shun and Yü, the other two sagacious presidents, left with us also some poems. Their works, together with other verses by following emperors and statesmen, may be found in our classics and official histories.

In the Chou Dynasty (1122–256 B.C.) poetry became more important, not only to individual and social life, but also to the government. Emperors used to travel over all the feudal states and to collect the most popular and typical poems or songs. The collection being then examined by the official historians and musicians, public opinion and the welfare of the people in the respective states would thus be ascertained and attested. In the ceremonies of sacrifice, inter-state convention, official banquet, and school and military exercises, various poems were sung and harmonized with music. Poetry in this period was not a special literary task for scholars, but a means of expression common to both sexes of all classes.

THE CLASSICAL POEMS

One of the five Confucian classics is the *Book of Poetry.* It is a selection of poems of the Chou Dynasty, classified under different types. This selection was made by Confucius out of the governmental collections of many states. It contains three hundred and eleven poems, all of high standard, both as literature and as music. Since the loss of the Confucian *Book of Music* during the period of the Great Destruction (221–211 B.C.) the musical significance of this classic can hardly be traced, but its literary value remains and the distinction of the classical poems, which can never be duplicated.

POEMS SINCE THE HAN DYNASTY

The classical poems were usually composed of lines of four characters, or words, with every other line rhymed. Lines were allowed, however, of more or fewer words. Under the reign of the Emperor Wu (140–87 B.C.) of the Western Han Dynasty new types of poetry were introduced; and the five-character and seven-character poems became popular and have dominated ever since. The Emperor himself invented the latter; while Li Ling and Su Wu, two of his statesmen-generals, wrote their verses in the former type. The number of characters of each line was uniform; no irregular line might occur. These two types were afterwards named the "ancient" or "unruled" poems. Nearly all poems before the T'ang Dynasty were in this form. The Emperor Wu introduced also the Po Liang style, which is a seven-character poem with every line rhyming in the last word.

Po Liang was the name of a pavilion in the Emperor's garden where, while he banqueted his literary attendants, each wrote one line to complete a long poem. This has been a favourite game among Chinese poets.

THE POEMS OF THE T'ANG DYNASTY

As many a dynasty in Chinese history is marked by some phase of success representing the thought and life of that period, the T'ang Dynasty is commonly recognized as the golden age of poetry. Beginning with the founder of the dynasty, down to the last ruler, almost every one of the emperors was a great lover and patron of poetry, and many were poets themselves. A special tribute should be paid to the Empress Wu Chao or the "Woman Emperor" (684–704), through whose influence poetry became a requisite in examinations for degrees and an important course leading to official promotion. This made every official as well as every scholar a poet. The poems required in the examination, after long years of gradual development, followed a formula, and many regulations were established. Not only must the length of a line be limited to a certain number of characters, usually five or seven, but also the length of a poem was limited to a certain number of lines, usually four or eight or twelve. The maintenance of rhymes, the parallelism of characters, and the balance of tones were other rules considered essential. This is called the "modern" or "ruled" poetry. In the Ch'ing or Manchu Dynasty the examination poem was standardized as a five-character-line poem of sixteen lines with every other line rhymed. This "eight-rhyme" poem was accompanied by the famous "eight-legged" literature (a form of literature divided into eight sections) as a guiding light for entrance into mandarin life.

The above-mentioned rules of poetry applied first only to examination poems. But afterwards they became a common exercise with "modern" or "ruled" poems in general. Chinese poetry since the T'ang Dynasty has followed practically only two forms, the "modern" or "ruled" form and the "ancient" or "unruled" form. A poet usually writes both. The "eight-rhyme" poem, however, was practised for official examinations only.

The progress of T'ang poetry may be viewed through a division into four periods, as distinguished by different styles and a differing spirit. There were, of course, exceptional works, especially at the transient points, and it is difficult to draw an exact boundary line between any two periods. The first period is approximately from A.D. 620 to 700, the second from 700 to 780, the third from 780 to 850, and the fourth from 850 to 900. The second period, corresponding to the summer season of the year, is regarded as the most celebrated epoch. Its representative figures are Li Po (705–762), the genie of poetry; Tu Fu, (712–720), the sage of poetry; Wang Wêi (699–759) and Mêng Hao-jan (689–740), the two hermit-poets, and Ts'en Ts'an (given degree, 744) and Wêi Ying-wu (about 740–830), the two magistrate-poets. The first period is represented by Chang Yüeh (667–730) and Chang Chiuling (673–740), two premiers, and by Sung Chih-wên (died 710) and Tu Shên-yen (between the seventh and the eighth centuries); the third, by Yuan Chên (779–832) and Po Chü-yi (772–846), two cabinet ministers, and by Han Yü (768–824) and Liu Tsung-yüan (773–819), two master *literati* more famous for their prose writing than for their verse; and the fourth, by Wên T'ing–yün (ninth century) and Li Shang-yin (813–858), the founders of the Hsi K'un school, and by Hsü Hun (given degree, 832) and Yao Hê (A.D. 9th century). All these poets had their works published in a considerable number of volumes. Secondary poets in the T'ang Dynasty were legion.

POEMS AFTER THE T'ANG DYNASTY

Since the T'ang Dynasty, poetry has become even more popular. Its requirement as one of the subjects in the governmental examinations has continued, for a thousand years, to the end of the last century, through all changes of dynasty. Many great poets have arisen during this time. Su Shih (1036-1101), Huang T'ing-chien (1050–1110), Ou-yang Hsiu (1007–1072) and Lu Yu (1125–1209), of the Sung Dynasty, are names as celebrated as those great names of the second period of the T'ang Dynasty. But people still honour the works of the T'ang poets as the model for ever-coming generations, though many of more varied literary taste prefer the Sung works.

Chao Mêng-fu (1254–1322) of the Yüan Dynasty and Yüan Hao-wên (1190–1258) of the Kin Dynasty were the shining stars of that dark age. Many poets of the Ming Dynasty, such as Liu Chi (1311–1375), Sung Lien (1310–1381), Li Tung-yang (1447–1516), and Ho Ching-ming (1483–1521) were very famous. Still greater poets lived in the Ch'ing Dynasty. Ch'ien Ch'ien-yi (1581–1664), Wu Wêi-yeh (1609–1671), Wang Shih-chêng (1526–1593), Chao Yi (1727–1814), Chiang Shih-ch'üan (1725–1784), Yuan Mêi (1715–1797), Huang Ching-jên (1749–1783), and Chang Wên-t'ao (1764–1814) are some of the immortals. Their works are by no means inferior to those in the previous dynasties.

Literature differs from science. It changes according to times and conditions, but shows, on the whole, neither rapid improvement nor gradual betterment. Later writings might appear to be more expressive and therefore more inspiring, but the dignity and beauty of ancient works are inextinguishable and even unapproached. This is especially true of poetry and of the T'ang poems, for the reason that during those three hundred years the thinking capacity and the working energy of all excellent citizens in the Empire were encouraged and induced to this single subject. Neither before nor after has there been such an age for poetry.

SELECTIONS OF THE T'ANG POEMS

Hundreds of collections and selections of T'ang poems have been published during the succeeding dynasties. Two compiled in the Ch'ing Dynasty are considered the best. One is the *Complete Collection of T'ang Poems* and the other is the *Three Hundred T'ang Poems.* These two have no similarity in nature and in purpose. The first is an imperial edition aiming to include every line of existing T'ang poetry: which amounts to 48,900 poems by 2,200 poets in 900 volumes. The second is but a small text-book for elementary students, giving only 311 better-known works by 77 of the better-known writers, the same number of poems as in the Confucian *Classic of Poetry.* This selection was made by an anonymous editor who signed himself "Hêng T'ang T'uêi Shih" or "A Retired Scholar at the Lotus Pool," first published in the reign of the Emperor Ch'ien Lung (1735–1795). The tide of this selection was based upon a common saying: "By reading thoroughly three hundred T'ang poems, one will write verse without learning."

In the preface the compiler assures us that "this is but a family reader for children; but it will hold good until our hair is white." This statement, as years have passed, has proved true.

The collection has always stood in China as the most popular volume of poetry, for poets and for the mass of the people alike. Even illiterates are familiar with the title of the book and with lines from it. Other selections may be of a higher standard and please scholars better, but none can compare with this in extensive circulation and accessible influence. [....]

VARIOUS POETIC REGULATIONS AND FORMS

There are more strict regulations in writing poems in Chinese than in any other language. This is because Chinese is the only living language governed by the following rules: First, it is made of individual hierographic characters; second, each character or word is monosyllabic; and third, each character has its fixed tone. Hence certain very important regulations in Chinese poetry are little considered or even unknown to the poetry of other languages. For instance, the avoidance of using a word twice, the parallelism of words of the same nature and the balancing of words of different tones, all need special preliminary explanation.

The first of these regulations is possible only in Chinese poetry. We find many long poems with hundreds or even thousands of characters, and not a single one repeated, as in the form of *p'ai-lü* or "arranged rule." The second means that all the characters of one line should parallel as parts of speech those of the next line; thus noun with noun, adjective with adjective, verb with verb, etc. Even in the same parts of speech, nouns designating animals should be parallel, adjectives of colour, numbers, etc. The third means that all the characters of a line should balance, in the opposite group of tones, those of the next line. There are five tones in the Chinese written language. The first is called the upper even tone; the second, the lower even tone; the third, the upper tone; the fourth, the departing tone; and the fifth, the entering tone. The first two are in one group, named " even tones," and the last three are in the other group and named "uneven tones." Thus, if any character in a line is of the even group, the character which balances with it in the next line should be of the uneven group, and vice versa.

These strict regulations, though very important to "modern" or "ruled" poems, do not apply to "ancient" or "unruled" poems. The ancient form is very liberal. There are but two regulations for it—namely, a limit to the number of characters in each line, five or seven; and rhyme on the last character of every other line. The seven-character "ancient" poem gives even more leeway. It may have irregular lines of more or fewer characters, and every line may rhyme as in the Po Liang style.

There are also, as in English, perfect rhymes and allowable rhymes. The perfect rhymes are standardized by an Imperial Rhyming Dictionary. In this dictionary all characters are arranged, first according to the five tones, and then to different rhymes. The two even tones have 30 rhymes; the third, 29; the fourth, 30; and the fifth, a very short sound, only 17. These rhymes are so grouped, following the old classical pronunciation, that some rhyming words may seem to the modern ear discordant. The allowable rhymes include words that rhymed before the standard was made. The "modern" poem must observe perfect rhymes; the "ancient" poem is permitted allowable rhymes. Again, the former should use only one rhyme of the even tones; the latter may use many different rhymes of different tones in one poem.

The "modern" poem has also its fixed pattern of tones. There are four patterns for the five-character poems and four for the seven-character poems. [....]

The first group of a "ruled poem" is named the "rising pair"; the second, the "receiving pair"; the third, the "turning pair"; and the fourth, the "concluding pair." In writing a "modern" or "ruled" poem many essential regulations are involved. They may be summed up in six rules:

1. Limitation of lines (four or eight, though the *p'ai-lü* or "arranged rule" poem may have as many lines as the writer likes).

2. Limitation of characters in each line (five or seven).

3. Observation of the tone pattern (the five-character four-line poems in old times did not observe this rule strictly).

4. Parallelism of the nature of words in each couplet (though the first and the last couplets may be exempted).

5. Selection of a single rhyme from the even tones and rhyming the last characters of alternate lines (the second, the fourth, the sixth, and the eighth lines; sometimes the first line also). The five-character four-line poems in the old days, however, were allowed rhymes from the uneven tones.

6. Avoidance of using a character twice unless deliberately repeated for effect.

Thus we see the great difficulty in writing a "modern" poem. But poets have always believed that the "modern" poem, though difficult to learn, is easy to write, while the "ancient" poem, though easy to learn, is very difficult to write well. Besides, the "modern" poem is constructed in a very convenient length. It enables the poet to finish his whole work while his thought is still fresh and inspiring; and, if necessary, he can express it in a series, either connected or separated. We find, ever since the T'ang Dynasty, most of the poets writing most of their poems in the "modern" forms.

CHINESE POETRY IN GENERAL

All the above statements treat only poems which are in Chinese called *shih.* This word is too narrow to correspond to the English word "poetry," which is more like the Chinese word *"yün-wên,"* or rhythmic literature, and yet *"yün-wên"* has a broader content, for it includes also drama. There are, however, many other kinds of *yün-wên* besides *shih,* not only drama, but poetry in general. [....]

In the later part of the Chou Dynasty two new types of poetry were originated; one is the *ch'u-ts'ü,* by Ch'ü Yüan (fourth century, B.C.), and the other *fu,* by Hsün K'uang (fourth century B.C.). They are both, though rhymed, called rhythmic prose, and have been much practised ever since. The latter is more popular and used to be a subject in the official examinations. Since the Han Dynasty, the *yüeh-fu,* or poem "written for music," has been introduced into literature....Because we do not sing them with their old music, which has vanished, they have practically lost their original quality, though still distinguished by title and style.

Another type of poetry, named *ts'ü,* was formulated in the second period of the T'ang Dynasty, but was not commonly practised until the last, or fourth, period. The Sung Dynasty is the golden age of the *ts'ü* poems and Li Ch'ing-chao and Chu Shu-chên, two woman poets, are the most famous specialists. This form is composed of lines irregular, but according to fixed patterns. There are hundreds of patterns, each regulated as to the number of characters, group of tones, etc. In the same dynasty the *ch'ü*, or dramatic song, the *t'an-ts'ŭ*, or string song, and the *ku-shu*, or drum tale, were also brought into existence. The next dynasty, the Yüan or Mongol Dynasty, is known as the golden age of these forms of literature. Professional story-tellers or readers are found everywhere singing them with string instruments or drums. Besides these, the *ch'uan-ch'i*, or classical play, the *chiao-pên*, or common play, and the *hsiao-tiao*, or folk-song, are all very popular.

There are numberless Chinese poems written in the revolving order, to be read back and forth. The most amazing poems in human history are the *Huêi-wên-t'ü* or the revolving chart, by Lady Su Huêi, of the Chin Dynasty (265–419), and the *Ch'ien-tzŭ-wên*, or thousand-character literature, by Chou Hsing-ssŭ, (fifth century A.D.) The former is composed of eight hundred characters, originally woven in five colors on a piece of silk, being a love-poem written and sent to her husband. General Tou T'ao, who was then guarding the northern boundary against the Tartar invasion. The characters can be read from different ends in different directions and so form numerous poems. Four hundred have already been found, some short and some very long. It is believed that there are still more undiscovered. The latter, made of a thousand different characters, was a collection of stone inscriptions left by the master calligrapher, Wang Hsi-chih. They had been but loose characters in no order and with no connexion, but were arranged and rhymed as a perfect poem by Chou Hsing-ssŭ. The same thousand characters have been made into poems by ten or more authors; and these marvels in the poetical world can never be dreamed of by people who speak language other than Chinese!

All these various forms under various names are not *shih* in the Chinese sense, but are poetry in the English sense. Each of them possesses its own footing in the common ground of Chinese poetry. To make any remarks on Chinese poetry at large, or to draw any conclusions from it, one must take into consideration not only the *shih*, but all the various forms. I sometimes hear foreigners, as well as young Chinese students, blaming Chinese poems as being too stiff or confined. They do not realize that some forms of Chinese poetry are even freer than English free verse. They also criticize the Chinese for having no long poems, as other races have, ignoring the fact that many *fu* poems are thousands of lines long, with tens of thousands of characters, and that many rhythmic historical tales fill ten or more volumes, each volume following a single rhyme.

KIANG KANG-HU
Peking, China, 1929

BIOGRAPHICAL NOTE
by Bob Holman and Margery Snyder

THE CLASSICAL CHINESE poet Li Po was both a rebel wanderer and a courtier. He is revered along with his contemporary, Tu Fu, as one of the two greatest Chinese poets.

LI PO'S EARLY LIFE
The great Chinese poet Li Po was born in 701 and grew up in western China, in Sichuan province near Chengdu. He was a gifted student, studied the classic Confucian works as well as other more esoteric and Romantic literature; by the time he was a young man he was an accomplished swordsman, practitioner of the martial arts and bon vivant. He began his wanderings in his mid-twenties when he sailed down the Yangtze River to Nanjing, studied with a Taoist master, and entered into a brief marriage with the daughter of a local official in Yunmeng. She evidently left him and took the children because he had not secured a government position as she hoped and instead had dedicated himself to wine and song.

IN THE IMPERIAL COURT
In his wandering years, Li Po had befriended the Taoist scholar Wu Yun, who praised Li Po so highly to the emperor that he was

invited to the court in Chang'an in 742. There he made such an impression that he was dubbed "the Immortal banished from heaven" and given a post translating and providing poetry for the emperor. He participated in the court revels, wrote a number of poems about events in court, and was renowned for his literary performances. But he was often drunk and outspoken and not at all suited to the strictures and the delicate hierarchies of court life. In 744 he was banished from court and went back to his wandering life.

WAR AND EXILE

After leaving Chang'an, Li Po formally became a Taoist and in 744 he met his great poetic counterpart and rival, Tu Fu, who said the two were like brothers and slept together under a single cover. In 756, Li Po was mixed up in the political upheaval of the An Lushan Rebellion and was captured and sentenced to death for his involvement. A military officer whom he had saved from court-martial many years before and who was by now a powerful general intervened and Li Po was instead banished to the far southwestern interior of China. He wandered slowly toward his exile, writing poems along the way, and in the end was pardoned before he got there.

LI PO'S DEATH AND LEGACY

Legend has it that Li Po died embracing the moon—late at night, drunk, in a canoe out on the river, he caught sight of the moon's reflection, leaped in, and fell into the watery depths. Scholars, however, believe he died from cirrhosis of the liver or from mercury poisoning that resulted from Taoist longevity elixirs.

Author of 100,000 poems, he was a nobody in a class-bound Confucian society and lived the wild poet's life long before the Romantics. About 1,100 of his poems are still in existence.

SOURCE: Bob Holman & Margery Snyder. "Li Po: One of China's Most Renowned Poets." ThoughtCo. https://www.thoughtco.com/poet-li-po-2725342.

www.ingramcontent.com/pod-product-compliance
Lightning Source LLC
Chambersburg PA
CBHW032047040426
42449CB00007B/1022